LEARNING
to live with
chronic
illness

5 Studies for Individuals or Groups

Lisa J. Copen

This book is dedicated to

My mom & dad
who always told me that I could do anything;

& my husband
who gives me unconditional love
and the freedom so that I can try.

Lisa J. Copen
Founder & Executive Director
Rest Ministries, Inc.
Serving people who live with chronic
illness or pain.
P.O. Box 502928, San Diego, CA 92150
858-486-4685
Toll-free 1-888-751-REST (7378)
website: www.restministries.org
email: rest@restministries.org

Published by Rest Ministries Publishers
Cover design JLC Productions

Contents

I Can't Do it Alone..5

I Feel So Guilty..9

Everything Is So Out of Control.....................17

My Body Image Is Hurting 23

How Do I Cope With This Depression?.........29

Study 1 _____

I Can't Do it Alone

"God knows exactly what it is that I need," Janelle tells her friends. "And He knew that I didn't need clean kitchen floors today!" Dirty kitchen floors and clean shower stalls are not often our priorities when we are just trying to make it through the basic tasks of the day while living with a chronic illness. Eventually, these things must be done, however, and sometimes we need to ask for help.

When we are diagnosed with a chronic condition, we become dependent on other people in a way that can be difficult in which to adjust. "I find myself in situations every day where I must ask for help," shares Janelle. "I allow people to open doors for me. I ask the grocery store checker to open the jar of whatever I purchase for dinner. I ask people to open, close, pull, push, twist, turn, reach, grab, tighten, loosen, lock and pour in the average twelve-hour day. Each time it becomes a little easier to ask for help than the last. Each time, however, I wish I was capable of doing it for myself."

Why is it so much easier to give help to others than it is to receive it? When we are able to help out friends by cooking a meal or running an errand, we receive great joy in knowing that we are being of assistance. When they try to return the favor though, we stammer in awkwardness, "That's really not necessary. I'm fine...really." Yet, deep down we know that we aren't fine; we know that we could really use the help. But it's often easier for us to deny this fact than it is to accept that we are no longer able to accomplish all that we did once upon a time.

Read Exodus 17: 8-13.

1. How was Moses able to hold up his hands for many hours?

2. Did Moses accept the help of his friends easily?

   What would have occured his Moses had not accepted the help of his friends?

3. Aaron and Hur held Moses' hands up—one on one side, one on the other—so that his hands remained steady till sunup" (v. 12). God's power was flowing through the fingertips of Moses, and yet God still allowed Moses' arms to become tired. Why do you believe God placed Moses in the situation where he had to accept help?

4. When is the last time you remember asking for help?

5. Jesus said "It is more blessed to give than to receive" (Acts 20:35b). Most of us feel more comfortable giving to others than we do receiving. Discuss why some people find it easier to ask for help than others. Which way you tend to be? Why do you believe you feel the way you do?

6. Can you think of some ways that God has blessed you when you have had to accept the help of others?

7. List five things you are currently trying to take care of that some one else could help you with if you would allow it.

1. _____

2. _____

3. _____

4. _____

5. _____

This week ...   ***Memorize I Thessalonians 2:4***

"We are not trying to please men, but God, who tests our hearts."

Choose at least two of the things you listed in question 7 that you are going to give up responsibility for this week and accept help.

(a) Task: _____
    Who are you going to ask help from?

    _____

(b) Task: _____
    Who are you going to ask help from?

    _____

Take time this week to receive the gift of assistance from those around you, both loved ones and strangers. People will receive great joy in being able to give you something that they know you need and you can give them the gift of appreciation.

At the end of the week, record how accepting help made you feel? Did it get any easier? Why or why not? (It will! Keep working on it.)

Study 2 _____

I Feel So Guilty

Who of us have not had a moment in which we've felt guilty?
When one has a chronic illness, daily living can be filled with a
multitude of guilty emotions. We feel guilty that our children
don't have a healthy parent. We feel guilty that we require use
of a wheelchair when we go to the summer fair. (If we even
go!) We feel guilty that doing the dishes and making the bed
has become less of necessity and more of a luxury.

"I think the hardest part of having a chronic illness was
the extreme fatigue that accompanied it," explains Deena. "I
was so exhausted all of the time that the house just fell apart. It
was a disaster, and seeing my husband trying to keep things up,
as I just lounged on the couch, made me feel worse. It wasn't
as if I was recovering from surgery or something with an
ending date. We didn't know how long it would go on. I
started to wonder if I would ever be able to raise my kids and
take care of my family. I felt like a horrible mother and wife."

John says, "Yeah, I was one of those guys who was
always helping someone move or build a fence. But when I
was diagnosed with multiple sclerosis that started to change. It
seemed like overnight I went from hiking and biking to
apologizing to my kids that we couldn't go camping for awhile.
It was tough. It was real tough to have to face the fact that I
wasn't going to be able to give my kids all of the opportunities
that I had planned. I wanted to be a dad, and to me a dad went
downhill skiing, shot hoops, and everything else. I felt guilty
that I wasn't going to be able to be the dad I wanted to be."

1. **Read Proverbs 16:18 & Romans 12:3.**

2. Often guilt is felt because we have high expectations of ourselves. How does Proverbs 16:18 & Romans 12:3 address the issue of pride and self-sufficiency?

3. Check the expectations that you have of yourself.
   _____ Never be a burden.
   _____ Don't ask for help.
   _____ Do as much as possible, even if it hurts.
   _____ Don't stop until I drop.
   _____ Provide healthy, well-balanced meals.
   _____ Don't hurt anyone's feelings; always please others.
   _____ Be responsible; remember things like birthdays.
   _____ Do everything for the holidays I did before I became ill.
   _____ Always be receptive to my spouse.
   _____ Never cry.
   Other _____
   Other _____

4. Oftentimes the expectations that we have of ourselves are unreasonable. Go back and put an "X" next to the expectations that are unreasonable.

5. When we have unreasonable expectations of ourselves, we begin to feel guilty. What causes you to feel guilty? Check each that applies.
   _____ I am always sick.
   _____ My illness runs the lives of my family members.
   _____ I don't feel like I have enough faith.
   _____ I am not able to care for my family as I would prefer.
   _____ I can't do physical activities with my friends or family.
   _____ My house is never really clean.

_____ I don't have people over often or invite company from out of town.
_____ I eat out too much because I have difficulties cooking.
_____ I don't exercise enough.
_____ I don't eat right.
_____ I should have seen a doctor sooner.
_____ I should have been more assertive about my treatment.
_____ I feel guilty that I feel resentment towards an event in my life that triggered the illness.
Other _____
Other _____
Other _____

Why do we put these unrealistic expectations on ourselves, causing us to then feel guilty? "I really didn't want anyone feeling sorry for me," says Bryan. "I didn't want the guys saying, 'Here, let me get that for you,' or wondering if they should invite me to go fishing or not." We are often sensitive to how people will respond to our illness and so we place high expectations on ourselves so that we can "appear normal."

We don't want the pity, the condolences, or the awkwardness. We'd prefer to avoid hearing people say things like, "I know if you just got more rest you would feel so much better," or "I know just what you are going through..." If we can cook a turkey dinner for the entire family, clean our own home and smile through all of it no one will be able to say, "She seems to be getting worse..."

There are other kinds of guilt.

(a) Socially - People say things that make us feel guilty.
"Your illness is caused by stress. If you would just take it easy..."
"Oh... So you have a housekeeper? Must be nice..."
"Boy, I wish I could just sit around at home all day."
"You're so lucky to not have to work."

(b) Spiritually - Your condition is blamed on your spiritual life.
   "If you would just... pray harder, read your bible more, ask for healing again, pray the right way..."

(c) New Age - Your condition is blamed on your past and unwillingness to work through the psychological aspects that are causing your illness.
   "You have the power to heal yourself, if you... think positive, meditate, do yoga, eat more vegetables, stop harboring negative thoughts and repressing memories."

6. Discuss how these comments make you feel guilty:

7. **Read Acts 17:28.** The apostle Paul emphasized that it is in God "we live and move and have our being."

When we put our worth into what we are able to do rather than who we are we set ourselves up for failure. It is in God that we find our value, rather than searching for it in what we can accomplish.

8. Share a time that you tried to do something with your own power and it failed. How did this make you feel?

Recall an instance when you gave something over to God and felt at peace, even though it didn't work out as you would have preferred.

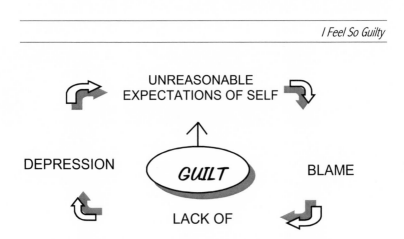

See how the cycle of guilt is a no-win situation? This is not how God wants us to live. Instead, He offers us grace.

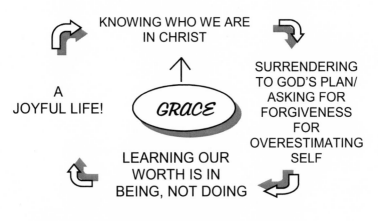

9. Circle above where you feel you are at right now.
    Draw a star where you want to be.
    Do you see how you must change your thought process and priorities in order to get there?

10. **Read 2 Timothy 1:9.** "Who has saved us and called us to
    a holy life--*not because of anything we have done* but
    because of his own purpose and grace. This grace was
    given us in Christ Jesus before the beginning of time."

    How does this verse make you feel about who you are?

11. **Read Ephesians 2:8.** "For it is by grace you have been
    saved, through faith--and this not from yourselves, it is the
    gift of God."

    How does this gift from God make you feel?

    If we continue to deny this gift and try to be self-sufficient,
    how do you believe that this makes God feel?

Once we are able to accept that it is through grace we are saved,
not works, we are able to ask God for forgiveness for
attempting to be self-reliant in the past and for our concern over
what others think. Galatians 1:10 says, "Am I now trying to
win the approval of men, or of God? ...If I were still trying to
please men, I would not be a servant of Christ."

12. Write out your commitment to not worry about what others
    think, and instead focus on Christ's unconditional love for
    you.

Dear God, _____

_____

_____

_____

_____

_____

_____

We can have a life filled with joy when we realize that because we are God's children, physical weakness is not something to be embarrassed about or ashamed of. We are to boast of it!

Paul said, "But he said to me, 'My grace is sufficient for you, for my power is made perfect in weakness.' Therefore I will boast all the more gladly about my weaknesses, so that Christ's power may rest on me," 2 Corinthians 12:9.

13. When Paul says that he will "boast of his weakness" what do you think he means by this?

How do you see yourself boasting of your weakness?

Memorize 2 Corinthians 9:8
"And God is able to make all grace abound to you, so that in all things at all times, having all that you need, you will abound in every good work."

This week when you find yourself having feelings of guilt, repeat the verse above to yourself and focus on the grace that God has provided you with so that you don't have to live with guilt.

✔ I started feeling guilty about _____

_____

but after refocusing on God's grace I felt_____

_____

✔ I started feeling guilty about _____

_____

but after refocusing on God's grace I felt_____

_____

✔ I started feeling guilty about _____

_____

but after refocusing on God's grace I felt_____

_____

Study 3 _____

Everything is so
Out of Control

Have you ever had one of those days where everything seems to be falling apart around you and you just can't seem to gain control over anything? We've all felt like one of those circus performers who spin the plates, except in our lives the plates don't always balance so well and they quickly start to fall. It's easy to believe that when we have God in our lives everything will run smoothly. Does not God promise peace and strength? (Psalms 29:11).

Yes, He does promise that He will provide us with peace and strength, but he does not promise us an easy journey. The difficulties that we will encounter in life make us depend on that peace. Without affliction we would have no reason to cry out to God for strength and endurance.

"I just feel like I am hanging on by a thread," explains Kelly. "Every day I fight to keep on moving forward, keep on smiling, and yet things seem to keep going wrong. Our finances, our plans for a home, everything seems to be running into roadblocks and I don't know what else to do. This would all be difficult enough if I was healthy, but when I don't have a single moment without pain, all of these other things are just too much! Where is God in all of this? Why won't he step in and give me some much-needed good news for a change?"

Illness has a way of coldly communicating that we don't have control over our lives. But who does? Does God? And if He does, why is He allowing us to suffer so much? If He's not going to step in, shouldn't we try to hold on to at least *some* control?

1. **Read Ecclesiastes 2:17-26.**

2. There are many things that we feel are out of our control. Check those below that apply to you.

_____ The physical changes taking place in my body.
_____ The mental changes taking place in my mind.
_____ The change in thought processes that I am having.
_____ The inability to make definite plans.
_____ The inability to have fun with friends.
_____ The inability to take care of my home.
_____ The inability to attend church or Christian fellowship.
_____ The inability to work.
_____ The inability to care for my children.
_____ The inability to have children.
_____ The inability to drive.
_____ The inability to cure myself.
_____ The inability to contribute financially or support myself.
_____ The inability to have people understand the seriousness of my condition.

Other: _____

_____

Other: _____

_____

"I feel most helpless when fatigue grabs me and shakes me like a rag doll and tosses me in a heap in the bed, unable to even change positions," says Debi. "Once, while trying to endure that 'drop-dead-bone-tired-exhaustion' that comes with illness, I was griping to God, telling Him... 'Father, I wish this was easier!' He promptly and lovingly replied 'I never said it would be easy, only *possible*.'"

3. What can we learn from Ecclesiastes 2: 17-23?

_____

_____

Life is difficult and when we encounter trials it can easy to wonder if God is really looking out for us and in control of our circumstances. In Act 27 the apostle Paul assures his men "I urge you to keep up your courage because not one of you will be lost, only the ship will be destroyed" (v. 23). God promises to take care of us, even when our "ship" is being knocked around and breaking apart.

Later Paul tells his men, "Keep up your courage, men, for I have faith in God that it will happen just as he told me. Nevertheless, we must run aground on some island" (v. 25). Paul wasn't pleased about what was in store for him. He even sounded a bit confused about God's plan, but he still responded with faith in God's power and his control over the situation.

4. When you feel as though you have no control over life's circumstances how do you respond?

(1). _____

(2). _____

(3). _____

(4). _____

(5). _____

5. On the list above, put an "X" beside those that are positive ways in which to respond. Do you often respond in a positive manner? A negative manner? Why do you believe this is so?

The Bible assures us that everything that is happening here on earth is "Father-filtered." There is nothing in our lives that God does not have control over.

"But our citizenship is in heaven. And we eagerly await a Savior from there, the Lord Jesus Christ, who, *by the power that enables him to bring everything under his control,* will transform our lowly bodies so that they will be like his glorious body" (Philippians 3:20, 21).

Even when it seems that God is not in control, we must trust His Word, and believe that He is all-powerful over our circumstances. Signs of trouble are not signs that God has surrendered control of our lives. Perhaps we are just "running aground on an island" for a bit. There are many verses that assure us that this is true:

- "In this world you will have trouble. But take heart! I have overcome the world," (John 16:33b).
- "For we are God's workmanship, created in Christ Jesus to do good works, which God prepared in advance for us to do," (Ephesians 2:10).
- "Dear friends, do not be surprised at the painful trial you are suffering, as though something strange were happening to you," (1 Peter 4:12).

List some other verses that promise God's control.

- _____

- _____

6. What makes you feel safe? Make a list of things that make you feel like you can survive, even in the midst of trials.

"When I am feeling overwhelmed with life's circumstances, I cling to Psalm 138:8," shares Candice. "'The Lord will fulfill his purpose for me; your love, O Lord, endures forever-- do not abandon the works of your hands.' I just say this verse over and over until I feel overcome by God's calmness. This verse explains how I feel because it is a confirmation that I know God is in control, and yet it ends with that little cry of desperation, which is where I'm at. You know—that feeling of 'I *know* you love me, Lord, but *pleeeease* don't abandon me!'"

Oftentimes when we are feeling afraid and overwhelmed by the circumstances in our life, it is because we are trying to take control over the situation, rather than give it to God. It is at this time that we have to surrender our worries and our concerns over to Him, and allow Him to heal our wounds. We will rarely get a clear explanation for why we must endure the trials that we encounter, but we are told to "Trust in the Lord with all your heart and lean *not* on your own understanding," (Proverbs 3:5).

7. What do the following verses tell us about trusting God with our lives?

Nahum 1:7 _____

_____

John 14:1 _____

_____

Romans 15:13 _____

_____

Psalms 118:8 _____

_____

This week ...

Memorize Jeremiah 29:11-13

"For I know the plans I have for you," declares the Lord, "plans to prosper you and not to harm you, plans to give you hope and a future. Then you will call upon me and come and pray to me, and I will listen to you. You will seek me and find me when you seek me with all your heart."

When those feelings of everything being out of control seem to overwhelm you, make a plan for how you will choose to cope with it in an effective and positive way.

For example, Greg says he chooses a verse to focus on and he also has a couple of things he can do to use as a distraction technique. It helps him not dwell on these thoughts so much if he can give it to God and then get on with other things. What is your plan?

My Plan

_____

_____

_____

_____

_____

_____

_____

Study 4 _____

My Body Image is Really Hurting

As an illness begins to enter into one's life, it enters into one's psychological being, as well as one's physical being. While others may not be able to see the physical changes taking place, one knows that they are there. Being in pain makes us more aware of our body in a way that an average person doesn't understand.

"When the joints my hand started to move out of place, suddenly I began to realize that the effects of my illness were more noticeable," explains Carey. "I could always put on a smile, pretending the pain wasn't bad, but when signs of my illness became more visible, I resented it. I just didn't want to have my great-grandmother's hands at the age of twenty-five."

For men other issues may arise. Perhaps they are unable to help friends move because they are unable to lift boxes or bend over. They begin to feel bad, not just about the illness, but how it is negatively affecting how they feel about their body. "When I became ill I really started to lose some weight," says Colin. "At first it was okay, but then I started to look too skinny—even sickly. No matter how hard I tried I couldn't seem to put the weight back on. When I looked in the mirror I didn't have any idea who the guy was who was looking back at me."

Whether it's weight loss, gain, changes in skin or joints, or other noticeable symptoms, many of us come to the point where the illness is not as invisible as it was once. Although the changes may barely be visible to those around us, in our minds they are a strong reminder that our body is getting worse. When this happens, how do we discover how to move forward and not become downcast?

1. **Read Psalm 139:14-16.**

   "I praise you because I am fearfully and wonderfully made. Your works are wonderful, I know that full well. My frame was not hidden from you when I was made in the secret place. When I was woven together in the depths of the earth, your eyes saw my unformed body. All the days ordained for me were written in your book before one of them came to be."

2. There are few people who are completely satisfied with their appearance. If you could change anything about your body, what would it be?

3. Reflect on the things you listed above and what Psalm 139:14-16 says. How does this make you feel about changing things about yourself?

4. Let's break this down and take a closer look at this verse.

"I praise you because I am fearfully and wonderfully made."
What does this verse mean to you?

"Your works are wonderful, I know that full well. My frame was not hidden from you when I was made in the secret place."
How does this verse make you feel?

"When I was woven together in the depths of the earth, your eyes saw my unformed body."
How is this verse reassuring?

"All the days ordained for me were written in your book before one of them came to be."
How does this make you feel in regard to your physical condition?

According to the Mayo Clinic, a negative body image can be related to low self-esteem, depression, sexual dysfunction, poor health habits, and in certain cases, psychiatric disorders. It can negatively affect feelings, behaviors, interpersonal relationships, decision-making ability, and day-to-day living.

Learning to accept your body takes practice and the understanding that there are some things about your looks you can't control. When we have an illness, we are faced with having to continually accept the changes; oftentimes, changes that we didn't think we would face until we were older (whatever age *older* is!)

"For most of my life I have been overweight," shares Miriam. "Then fourteen years ago I made a whole-hearted effort and lost twenty-five pounds to reach my goal weight. Seven years later I was diagnosed with fibromyalgia. I began taking an anti-depressant to help with my sleep difficulties. The drug, the fact that I can't always exercise, and that I sometimes eat for comfort from my pain, has caused me to gain over twenty-five pounds. I don't feel very good about my body anymore. I am beginning to lose the confidence in myself that losing weight had given me. I haven't given away all my 'skinny' clothes because I tell myself that someday I will get back in them. In my heart, though, I know it would be such a big battle and I just don't have the energy for it!"

If you are unhappy with your body, you aren't alone. Even those is Biblical times felt unrest with their body. "My back is filled with searing pain; there is no health in my body," (Psalms 38:7).

Recently *Psychology Today* magazine found that 56 percent of women and 43 percent of men surveyed were dissatisfied with their overall appearance, and two-thirds of the women and over half of the men were dissatisfied with their weight. A psychological study in 1995 found that three minutes spent looking at models in a fashion magazine caused 70 percent of women to feel depressed, guilty, and shameful.

5. Are we too concerned with how we look? Write out Philippians 3:19:

Paul also tells us to look forward to receiving our new body. "We eagerly await a Savoir from heaven, the Lord Jesus Christ, who by the power that enables him to bring everything under his control, will transform our lowly bodies so that they will be like his glorious body" (v. 21).

6. **Read 1 Corinthians 6: 19-20.** "Do you know that your body is a temple of the Holy Spirit who is in you, whom you have received from God? You are not your own. You were bought at a price. Therefore, honor God with your body."

There are days most of us look in the mirror and think, "Honor *this* body? Does God really expect that?" We are at home with our body, and yet also at war with it. How can we be expected to honor it when it has turned against us so aggressively? Why does God ask us to honor our body?

Our body is not really ours, but we are responsible for it. "It's like leasing a car," laughs Cheri. "I am responsible for how I treat it until I get to turn it in—only God's already paid the sticker price." Debi shares, "I used to be extremely angry with my body because my illnesses place limitations on my activities, but I am learning to lean on God during the weakest times. He has told me that His strength is made perfect in weakness and that His grace is sufficient for me."

7. List some ways that you could honor God with your body?

(a) _____

(b) _____

(c) _____

(d) _____

8. What is currently preventing you from doing these things?

9. It's easy to get caught up in the world's standards, especially when it comes to our appearance. "Am I now trying to win the approval of men, or of God? ...If I were still trying to please men, I would not be a servant of Christ," (Galatians 1:10). 2 Corinthians 4:10 says, "We always carry around in our body the death of Jesus, so that the life of Jesus may also be revealed in our body." How do these verses add a new perspective to your body image?

This week ...

Memorize Acts 17:28

"It is in God we live and move and have our being."

This week when you put on clothes that don't fit, when your leg starts to shake as you walk, when just lying in bed creates pain, repeat Acts 17:28 above to yourself as a reminder that we must not measure ourselves against the world's standards, but strive to find our value in being a child of God.

At the end of the week reflect back on how much of a difference it made to your body image by repeating Acts 17:28 to yourself during those moment of "body frustrations."

My Body Image Diary

_____

_____

_____

_____

_____

_____

_____

_____

_____

_____

_____

_____

Study 5 _____

How do I Cope with this Depression?

"When I was depressed and I looked out my window, the landscape looked absolutely flat and colorless," says Sherry, a woman with scleroderma. "As I began to feel better about myself and to experience my own inner beauty and worth, this movement was mirrored in the way I saw the outside world. Now when I look out my window, I see depth, dimension and color that I never knew existed. Getting out from under depression literally changed my life."

Who wouldn't be depressed by having a chronic illness? Isn't it a normal reaction? In the Bible, even the king asked Nehemiah, "Why does your face look so sad when you are not ill?" (Nehemiah 2:2). For a time depression may be a normal response to chronic illness, but when a few months have passed and you are still feeling depressed, it's time to look for a way to move on.

Florence Littauer, author of *Blow the Black Clouds Away,* notes, "I've learned that justified depression is the worst type to overcome. When we can conclude that 'anyone would be depressed in my circumstances,' there is little impetus to move."

"I'm so tired of that feeling of desperation," shares Tim. "I can't help but wonder if my wife and kids would be better off without me. I know that God doesn't wish for me to live this way, but I don't know what to do. I even doubt my faith, because if I really *had* faith, I wouldn't be feeling like this, right?"

Most of us have had at least a brief time in our life when we felt hopeless. Let's take a closer look at depression and what we can do when we get into these pits of despair.

1. Read 2 Corinthians 4:8.

Just because you are dealing with depression does not mean that there is something wrong with your spiritual life.   True, there are times that depression *is* a result of sin, but *not* always. If you are a Christian who has a chronic illness, you are probably already aware of the theological misinterpretations people have about healing and physical ailments. Comments like "Real Christians don't get depressed..." can hurt, because the person is implying that you are not a real Christian. That stings, especially if it comes from someone who holds authority.

6.   Describe how you react when you feel "struck down..."

3. Describe a time that you felt "destroyed." What was it that made you move forward from this point?

4. Often people who are depressed feel isolated in the emotions that they are encountering. No one seems to understand the pain that they are going through and since they usually "look healthy" depressed people tend to feel hypocritical, as though they are "faking their way through life." Have you ever felt this way?

If you answered "yes," you aren't alone. Despite the fact that everyone around you may seem happy and content, 15 percent of all adults have symptoms of depression—over 50 million people, and two-thirds of them are not receiving any treatment.

5. Faith *does* make a difference. A recent study at Duke University found that 54 percent of the depressed participants recovered from their depression during the nearly year-long study and that the strength of a person's inner religious faith dramatically seemed to influence how quickly recovery occurred. Does this make you feel hopeful or not?

6. Some people have found strength in Paul's example. "I have learned in whatever state I am in to be content." How does this verse make you feel in your circumstances? Comforted? Frustrated? Angry? List the emotions you have when you read this.

7. **Read 1 Kings 19:1-8.** Summarize the passage here:

8. Even Christians become despondent and cry out, "I've had it! That's enough!" Elijah wanted to die. 'I have had enough, Lord,' he said. 'Take my life." Have you ever felt the temptation to take your life?

What was it that made you reconsider?

Like Elijah, by faith we recognize the Lord is the giver and taker of life. Our life rests in his hands. He will deliver us from life's trials when the time is right, if we wait on him.

9. What can we learn from this passage?

(a) We cannot run from life's troubles.
(b) We must come to grips with what causes our despondency and unwillingness to accept the situation that confronts us and a weakness in trusting the Lord to bring us through it.
(c) The Lord watched over Elijah through the stresses of his life and his despondency. He sent an angel to minister to his needs.
(d) _____
(e) _____
(f) _____

(g) _____

(h) _____

(i) _____

10. Can you think of a time when you were in despair and God
    sent a person, situation, or revelation that was your
    "angel?" Share about it below.

11. How can we get out of our depression? Each person is an
    Individual and so we cannot answer that question with one
    simple conclusion. However, we can take a look at what
    God's prescription was for Elijah's despair.

1 Kings 19:5 _____

_____

1 Kings 19:6 _____

_____

1 Kings 19:12 _____

_____

1 Kings 19:15_____

_____

12. 1 Kings 19:15 is a way of God saying "Get on with it... You may feel struck down, but you are not destroyed... Life goes on!" Be honest with yourself: What are some ways that you need to "get on with it?"

For some, part of getting on with it is to seek out professional help. Clinical depression is a serious matter and often requires treatment with medication and possibly counseling too. See a physician about your depression and discuss treatment options.

Just because you are feeling a bit down, however, does not mean that you need to be treated with medication. If your physician is quick to give you medication just because you mentioned you're feeling a bit down, don't run out and fill the prescription. It may be wise to talk with a psychiatrist first. We have become a society that quickly treats any ailment with medications, oftentimes unnecessarily. The last thing you need is an interaction between medications or more side effects.

As Christians, it's important to recognize that we are not going to have a life full of bliss and happiness at every turn. When we are depressed and at rock bottom and seek out God, He will surround us with His comfort and lead us to a better place. Sometimes we need to feel that dependence on God and benefit from knowing that He turned our life around.

At the same time, don't discount treatment of medications, just because you are a Christian. Depression is a serious illness and should be treated as such.

For a Christian counselor in your area contact:
- **The American Association of Pastoral Counselors (AAPC)**
  1-800-225-5603 or website at http://www.aapc.org/
- **Christian Counseling Directory**
  website at: http://www.fishernet.com/counslng/Directory. htm

---

This week ...

Memorize Psalms 42:11
Why are you downcast, O my soul? Why so disturbed within me? Put your hope in God, for I will yet praise him, my Savior and my God.

Psalms 119:147
I rise before dawn and cry for help; I have put my hope in your word.

This week take some time to do a word study in the Bible. Look up some of the many verses (over 150) that contain the word "hope."

Write them out on index cards and place them all over your house so every time you begin to feel overwhelmed with feelings of self-doubt and fear you will remember that your hope is in the Lord.

Rest Ministries, Inc.

Serving people who live with chronic illness or

Rest Ministries, Inc. exists to serve people who live with chronic illness or pain, by providing spiritual, emotional, relational and practical support. Rest Ministries equips churches in the United States & beyond to minister to and with the chronically ill. **www.restministries.org**

Log onto our web site for free daily devotionals, articles, chats, discussion groups, prayer requests and much more.

HopeKeepers® Magazine

Designed with your specific needs in mind, *HopeKeepers* will encourage you on your Christian walk while you live with chronic illness and pain. Practical tools and inspiration make this a "can't miss magazine!"

- Articles about the things that matter to you: feelings, friends, family, finances and faith
- Updates on HopeKeepers® Groups & volunteers
- Q/A with a Christian doctor
- Caregivers column
- Tools to become a strong advocate for quality health care.
- Published every other month, 64 pages

www.MyHopeEndures.com

Join us for Hope Endures Radio Podcast where Lisa interviews special guests each week! 30-minute and 5-minute episodes available to download, listen online or call by phone!

So You Want to Start
A Chronic Illness/Pain Ministry
Learn how to:

- Run a small group.
- Educate the church about the social issues of illness.
- Address the issue of healing.
- Show people you care.
- Know what to say and what not to say.
- Answer the "whys" that come up in your group.
- Find resources for your group.
- Encourage people to participate.
- Determine the need in your church for a chronic illness/pain ministry.
- Define what chronic illness/pain ministry will be for you and your church. *70-page manual, just $15.00*

Start a HopeKeepers ministry in your church!

A HopeKeepers start-up kit includes:

· 1-year subscription to HopeKeepers® Magazine
· 5 copies of *When Chronic Illness Enters Your Life*
· 1 copy of *So You Want to Start a Chronic Illness/Pain Ministry* 70-page manual
· Flyers, meeting announcements, press releases for your church bulletin and newsletter., *Connections* CD Rom of 1000+ health resources
· Consulting with Rest Ministries founder, Lisa Copen, about the specific needs for your church *& much more*
Download a FREE HK Info Packet Online

Educating churches on how they can best serve the chronically ill, we are pleased to be presenting at churches and conferences. We discuss the issues of healing, what to say and not say to a chronically ill person, and the invisibility of illness and pain. Don't miss out on this exciting new ministry that is available for your church.

ORDER ONLINE www.restministries.org

Your Comments

We are always interested in hearing from you! Whether you would like to share your story or sorrows, we read each letter. Your comments help us shape the ministry and direct the magazine articles and Bible studies to be what you are looking for. With your permission, your comments may be included. Please include:

- your name
- your address
- is permission granted to quote you?

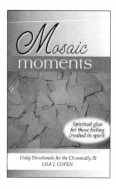

Mosaic Moments:
Devotions for the Chronically Ill

Over 200 devotionals from Rest Ministries founder Lisa Copen and your other favorite writers from Rest Ministries online daily devotionals. A wonderful gift for a non-believer who is struggling to make sense of it all, it includes an invitation to give your heart to Christ. We wrote this book because we wanted people to have a "real" and "raw" expression of what it's like to live with chronic illness—but also know the Lord. Pain is never easy—and this book doesn't say it is—but it's certainly better when one has someone to comfort them in the darkest moments

Price... $14

"I am so thankful to be able to offer *Mosaic Moments* as a resource to those who struggle with chronic pain and illness. Rarely are there words to convey my heartfelt concerns for suffering. With *Mosaic Moments* I am able to share a spiritual cup of cold water. It offers words of loving and caring I believe Jesus Himself would share." **Julie Russell, R.N., Parish Nurse, Stephen Minister**

Be sure to check us out on the web!
http://www.restministries.org

About the Author

Lisa Copen founded *Rest Ministries, Inc.* in 1997 after four years of living with a chronic illness (rheumatoid arthritis). Although she has found that God's plan for her life is much different than she expected, she intends to share her experiences in order to comfort others. It's no surprise that she bases the mission of her ministry on 2 Corinthians 1:4. "He comforts us whenever we suffer. That is why whenever other people suffer, we are able to comfort them by using the same comfort that we have received from God."

Lisa is the author of *Mosaic Moments: Devotionals for the Chronically Ill, Why Can't I Make People Understand?, When Chronic Illness Enters Your Life* (bible study), *So You Want to Start a Chronic Illness/Pain Ministry: 10 Essentials for Making it Work,* and *A Woman's Health Record-keeping Journal.* Rest Ministries is an affiliate of Joni and Friends. Lisa speaks about chronic illness/pain ministry at churches and special events. She lives in San Diego, CA with her husband, Joel and son, Joshua.

National Invisible Chronic Illness Awareness Week

Did you know nearly 1 in 2 people in the USA live with a chronic condition? And 96 percent of the illnesses are invisible! National Invisible Chronic Illness Awareness Week, held annually in September, is a designated time worldwide, in which people who live with chronic illness, those who love them, and organizations are encouraged to educate the general public, churches, health-care professionals, and government officials about the effects of living with a disease that is not visually apparent. For more information visit www.invisibleillness.com or contact Rest Ministries, the sponsor of this week at 888-751-7378.

Order Form

_____ *Why Can't I Make People Understand?* $12
_____ *Mosaic Moments: A Devotional for the Chronically Ill* $14
_____ *Beyond Casseroles: 505 Ways to Encourage a Chronically*
      Ill Friend .... $6 each or 3 for $15
_____ *So You Want to Start a Chronic Illness/Pain Ministry:*
      10 Essentials For Making it Work $15.00

Bible Studies
_____ *When Chronic Illness Enters Your Life* $6.50
_____ *Learning to Live with Chronic Illness* $6.50

❑   I would like to make a gift to *Rest Ministries* in the amount of _____.
❑   I would like to partner with *Rest Ministries* & I pledge to give _____
    each month. * *Rest Ministries, Inc. is a 501(c)(3) nonprofit. Your gift is
    tax-deductible.*
❑   I am interested in starting a HopeKeepers Group for people who live with
    chronic illness or pain. **Send me a HopeKeepers information packet.**

POSTAGE $1-$9.99 = $3.50; $10-$29.99 = $6.50; $30-$49.99 = $9.25;
$50-$74.99 - $13.00; $75-100 = $14; 100+ = 15% of purchase

TOTAL Purchases/Gifts: .... $_____
California residents add 7.75% to purchase (not donation) ..... $_____
TOTAL: .... $_____
_____ Include check made payable to Rest Ministries
_____ Charge my: ❑ Visa ❑ Mastercard
Card #

Send to: Rest Ministries, Inc., P.O Box 502928, San Diego, CA 92150

Expiration date:_____
Cardholder's signature *(required)* _____
Name: _____
Address: _____
City/State/Zip _____
Phone number: _____
Email_____

❑   *Please sign me up for HopeNotes, the weekly email updates*